IT'S ALL ABOUT THE IDEA

C000144948

BY TOM TUKE-HASTINGS

Published by The British Business School
Copyright © The British Business School 2016

Thomas Tuke-Hastings has asserted his moral right under the Copyright,
Designs and Patents Act, 1988, to be identified as the author of this work.

All rights reserved. This book is copyright material and must not be copied, reproduced,
transferred, distributed, leased, licenced or publicly performed or used in any way except as
specifically permitted in writing by the publisher, as allowed under the terms and conditions
under which it was purchased or as a strictly permitted by applicable copyright law.

Any unauthorised distribution or use of this text may be a direct infringement of the
author's or publisher's rights and those responsible may be liable in law accordingly.

A CIP catalogue record for this book is available from the British Library.

ISBN 978-0-9935365-0-2

www.BritishBusiness.School

IT'S ALL ABOUT THE IDEA

SO WHAT'S THE BIG IDEA?

Change how you bring creativity into your workplace in one year.

With 52 steps, this book gets you to focus on one step per week, changing the way you work and how you view creativity.

The idea is to read the book through and then implement one section per week. Focus on it on the Monday morning and evaluate the difference it has made on the Friday afternoon.

At the bottom of every page is a URL that links to the worksheet for that week, which you can print out and fill in. Whether on your own or as a team, you will find that by working through this, you will get better at the creative process. As you pick up the different techniques, they will become second nature, giving yourself and your team the edge. Think of it as a buffet, some of the ideas will work better for you than others. It's not an all or nothing, cherry pick the bits that work for you.

A.
GET SET FOR FOR SUCCESS

"Whether you think that you can, or that you can't, you are usually right"

Henry Ford

WEEK

1

PICK YOUR TARGET

A big idea without a target is just a big dream

The first step is setting your objective.

What do you want to achieve?

This is normally quite commercial. Launching a new product, raising sales or changing how people feel about a company or product are good examples. The days of saying it is good for the brand are gone. It is not enough just to get people talking; you need a strong and well-defined objective.

Always keep your objective in mind and test your ideas against this. Does the idea or the activation help get you one step closer to your objective? If not, why are you doing it? Having a clear objective helps you protect your ideas and make them true. If the idea starts getting eroded and changed, it might be that you are going off target. Things change and no plan survives first contact, but make sure you are making changes for the right reasons rather than just watering down your idea. Beware of design by committee as it usually weakens your ideas. By testing against your objectives, you know that you are doing the right thing.

"Obstacles are those frightful things you see when you take your eyes off your goal"
Henry Ford

www.BritishBusiness.School/BK0101

WEEK
2

WHAT DOES SUCCESS LOOK LIKE?

To check you are really clear about your objectives, ask the simple question: **"What does success look like?"** This can be for you or for your **"client"**, internal or external. If you can deliver this, then you and your client will be happy. If you get stuck working out what success is, ask some **W** questions.

- **Who?** *Who are the audience you need to hit?*
- **What?** *What are you trying to achieve?*
- **Where?** *Where do you want this to be done?*
- **When?** *When does it need to be done by?*
- **Why?** *Why are you doing this and how do you want people to feel once it is done?*
- **How?** *How would you like to achieve this?*
- **How much?** *What is the budget and the business case?*

"Success is the sum of small efforts - repeated day in and day out"
Robert Collier

WEEK
3

WHO DO
YOU THINK
THEY ARE?

You need to be absolutely clear about your target audience. Your strategy will be very different if you're trying to connect with 100 or 100,000 people, teenagers or adults and local or international audiences. **Define your market segment, your targets and your numbers. Don't waste your time and resources on people who don't (or won't) listen.** If you target 10% of the population and it is the wrong 10%, you are not going to do very well.

Once you are clear about your objectives and your target audience, you should have the beginnings of a pretty good brief. Now you just need a big idea…

" *Professor Porsche, in reply to an accusation that most people did not like his adverts, pointed out that most people could not afford his cars"*

WEEK
4

TIME FOR A
SHEEP DIP

If you are trying to come up with ideas about something, **you need to immerse yourself** in the topic. You need to have data and details to get the best ideas.

Surround yourself with information, pictures, stories and the competition. Get to know the market and look at the landscape. Only then you can get inside the skin of the project.

You need to get in the mind-set of your audience. It can be really simple. For a youth brand, we went to universities and gave our target market disposable cameras and some money. We asked them to spend the money on magazines and things they liked doing. From the magazines they tore out bits they were interested in and took photos of them doing the things they enjoyed. This very quickly gave us a huge bank of images that brought to life what our target market were interested in across the country.

"You can't use up creativity. The more you use, the more you have"

Maya Angelou

WEEK

5

SO WHAT MAKES UP A BIG IDEA?

So what is a big idea? What does it break down into?

*At a basic level, there is always the **core idea, the peripheral elements and the red thread** (or blue/ green/ yellow thread, it's your thread, so it should be in your colour).*

The core idea is the soul of the project. It is what you are doing and epitomises the idea. This is then normally augmented by peripheral ideas, the additional bits that make it better and interact with different audiences. The red thread is the glue, it is what takes you from A to B. You use it to check that you are doing things for the right reasons and that you hit your objectives.

So the first thing you need is your business objective. Refine this until it is clear. Then apply your audience. Who do you want to connect with and when?

You then develop your big idea, which becomes the red thread that links the whole way through the project from start to finish, keeping it on track and always attached to the business objective to ensure you hit it. Don't get so lost in the big idea that you forget the brief, that is why the red thread has to be linked to the objective.

Big ideas are fragile and need protecting. It is hard work, as with multiple external stakeholders there are people who want to change and dilute the idea. There are times when you do need to amend the idea, but it needs to be for the right reasons.

"A new idea is delicate. It can be killed by a sneer of a yawn; it can be stabbed to death by a joke, or worried to death by a frown on the right person's brow"

Charles Brower

www.BritishBusiness.School/BK0105

WEEK
6

HOW MUCH SPACE IS IN YOUR HARD DRIVE?

The world is a busy place and as our lives become ever fuller, most people (myself especially) can't remember everything.

We forget and misplace things. If you come up with a great idea or an element for one, write it down.

To live up to this, I have included some blank pages at the end of the book, so if something pops into your head as you read this, or you feel the beginnings of an idea, jot it down.

Start an ideas book. I have a lot of notebooks; they litter my house and are covered in scrawled diagrams, notes and ideas. There is one beside my bed that I use if I wake up in the night with an idea, separate ones for different projects and small ones to take with me.

Make sure yours is different from your workbook (if you have one) and use it. Draw, scribble and dream. Every now and then look back through it and you will be amazed by the quality of the ideas, as well as their ability to kick off other ideas.

Take advantage of digital options: write emails to yourself, use the notes function on your phone, or explore the huge variety of apps out there. The drawing programs are getting better and better.

I love sketching with pen and paper, but also really enjoy Paper by Fifty Three on iPad which lets me produce much better images than I can with traditional materials. Also, sharing is just a click away. Find out what works for you and enjoy it.

"I strongly believe that there are those who forget and those who write things down"

Tom Tuke-Hastings

WEEK
7

THINK
BIG

PLAN AND
PLAN NOT
TO PLAN

The market moves so fast that if you blink, you have missed it. To win you need to be opportunistic. Some people take advantage of these moments and win big, while others are left only to muse on what might have been.

Oreos got a lot of coverage for commenting on the blackout at the 2013 Super Bowl, while others were too slow to react. The way that they managed to do that was to have the right people in the room, with the authority to move in case something did happen.

For your big idea, you might need to be prepared to act opportunistically. There should be a structure so you know what you can do and a red phone line for sign off. Budget should be made available - we put it down as SWATU (Something Will Always Turn Up). This means that when things happen, you are ready to take advantage of them.

I like to take this a step further. We can plan for some things we know are going to happen, even if we don't know the exact date: a royal baby, snow or adverse weather and big events in popular sports. We know these things will happen, even if we don't know exactly when, so you can plan for them, e.g. in sports, one side will win, so prepare for both.

Of course, when it's a global media event, everyone is ready, so cut-through is hard. But there are hundreds of other opportunities - a new craze, a last minute cancellation, a big mistake by the competition. These things happen with surprising regularity. If you look through one weeks' worth of papers, there will be something that you could have jumped on, but chances are you didn't. You need to be fast to do this and you need to embrace your inner entrepreneur. You need to be flexible enough to respond and you need to take the time, even with the seconds slipping by, to make sure you get the most out of it.

"Realize that ultimate success comes from opportunistic, bold moves which by definition, cannot be planned"

Ross Johnson

www.BritishBusiness.School/BK0107

WEEK
8

THE
HISTORY
OF IDEAS

Ideas are key to the entire human race, they have driven us from living in trees to the top of the food chain.

We think naturally of Steve Jobs and James Dyson, but big ideas have driven our world in so many different ways.

The first use of tools was a huge idea. Looking back, the idea of picking up a stick and using it is simple, but at the time it was amazing. As for crushing rocks and heating them to extract metal, even now with all our knowledge, I doubt that many people could do this without being told what rocks to use and how to heat them. As history has whizzed forward, people have invented and innovated beyond the wildest dreams of the generation before. A lot is trial and error and history is full of stories of discoveries by luck, from penicillin to stainless steel.

We continue to innovate at a massive pace and consider ourselves to be in an age of ideas when we are moving forward at lightning pace.

Will innovators continue to build on our knowledge? Certainly. And in an age of crowd funding from sites such as Kickstarter.com it has all changed. A normal person with a good idea can get it funded to bring it to market and create a viable product and business. Once only the preserve of large companies with big Research and Development budgets, this might be the new American dream.

There are two things to take from this. Firstly that ideas are often seen as ridiculous and bound to fail; until they become so part of our day to day life that we can't think how we lived without them. The second is to take an interest in the past. Ideas that did not work before might now. It might have been that an idea was ahead of it's time, and the right it's time might be now.

"If I have seen further it is by standing on the shoulders of Giants"

Isaac Newton

www.BritishBusiness.School/BK0108

B.
GENERATING IDEAS

"Why, sometimes I've believed as many as six impossible things before breakfast"

Lewis Carroll

WEEK
9

THE
IDEA
TRIGGER

So you have an objective, you have an audience and now you are ready to come up with a **big idea:** So how do you get in the creative mood?

Environment can play an important role.

Once you have met the minimum physical requirements (comfortable, not too hot or cold) much of the rest is mental. Many authors have rituals that give them a strong mental signal that it is work time and the ideas start flowing. Using a certain pen, special ink or a particular time of day gets them in the mood. I always write with turquoise ink when working on ideas and making idea notes.

So what were you doing the last time you had a big idea? You might need to find your mental place by staring out of a window or playing with desk toys, it could be that a plain white space free of distraction is more to your taste. Think about what has worked for you before. Could this be the location or mental cue you need, to come up with your next big idea?

"The object isn't to make art, it's to be in that wonderful state which makes art inevitable"

Robert Henri

www.BritishBusiness.School/BK0109

WEEK
10

BEANBAGS
DON'T
MAKE YOU
CREATIVE

Bean bag rooms, the poster child of creativity in the 90s, **were popular with start-ups and companies like Google.** They were places where creatives would hang out and do their thing.

Not that everyone was sure what their thing was. In reality however, you don't need these to be creative. You don't need to wear skinny jeans, overly colourful clothes, grow a beard or subject your hair to a cut that you will look back on with amazement and distress.

Creativity comes from within and everyone has it. You just need to unlock it and how you use it. From the suited and booted in the boardroom to the flip flop wearing start-up, there is a huge amount of creativity out there waiting to be unlocked.

A change of scene is often a good thing, it can be as simple as going out for a coffee or sitting in a park. Some people are inspired by music, cooking or buildings. New environments can mean new ideas.

With companies struggling and times being harder, we can't all afford the space or the decor to build a separate idea space, so don't. Work out how to be creative in your existing space or to go to a public space that inspires you. Being creative is not about trying to turn you into someone else. You can be creative as you are, use your skills and how you approach life to make your own creative style.

"Creativity takes courage"
Henri Matisse

www.BritishBusiness.School/BK0110

WEEK
11

AN OCEAN
OF PAPER

A great way to get things moving is to put it on paper. Paper is wonderful stuff and even **those who find drawing difficult can use words and basic shapes to sketch out what they want to get across. You can pile it up, tear it up and pass it on.**

Use big sheets of paper to dump ideas and doodles. Keep using lots of it and sort it into relevant topics, with anything that is relevant or interesting. Don't be discriminating at first, the aim here is to get a big first cut that keeps you moving.

When you have run dry of ideas, cherry pick the good bits and put what is not working to one side. When you have your very best bits together, clear away the clutter and redraw and define these until you have a selection of easily understandable ideas.

You now have a great starting position to explain your outline idea to others. You might need to tidy it up, but the aim of this is to create ideas and develop them to a point where they can be easily explained to other people.

"Drawing makes you see things clearer, and clearer and clearer still, until your eyes ache"

David Hockney

WEEK
12

DREAM BIG, MAKE SMALL

Think big and dream big, we are after all **talking about big ideas.** If you shoot at the floor, you will hit it. If you shoot at the stars, you might not always hit them, but there are all sorts of interesting things on the way down that you might get.

It is always easier to scale down a big idea and end up with a quality product than trying to make a small idea big. A big idea gives something for everyone to get behind and believe in.

Have you been unable to think up an idea because there is not enough budget to do anything interesting? Start thinking of what you would do if there were no limits, then come up with clever ways to make it cheaper or scale it down.

"Follow your dreams, they know the way"
Kobe Yamada

www.BritishBusiness.School/BK0112

WEEK
13

LOOKING WITH YOUR EYES

It won't surprise you to hear that I am a visual person. I find it a **great way to share ideas** and to come up with them.

Men trust their ears less than their eyes.

Sometimes when I am looking for inspiration, I browse the subject I am looking at on Google. So far so normal, but I tend to use Google images and flit through pages very quickly. This helps give a great overview very quickly and get in the mind-set to start visualising other ideas. There are lots of visual resources out there from Google to Flikr. Using visual research changes the way you see topics.

Mood boards have been around for ages, but with the digital revolution, it is now easier than ever to create them and look at different images and inspirations. We can share them at the click of a button, whether it is to the other side of the office or the other side of the world. Pinterest.com is a great scrapbook tool for collating ideas and allows a myriad of different images and influences to be put together for very easing sharing.

"I take a simple view of life. It is keep your eyes open and get on with it"

Herodotus

www.BritishBusiness.School/BK0113

WEEK
14

Z Z z Z

DREAM
TIME

Ideas are not a standard **nine to five** job (what is anymore?).

It is very important to retain the skill to dream. *This is often no more than allowing yourself to do so and finding the time to do it.*

Time is one of the hardest things to get hold of in our busy lives. We have very little down time, so you need to be clever to find the time. Look to the gaps. Commuting can be a useful time to do this; you can close your eyes and let your mind drift away (but only on public transport – please don't do this if you are driving). When exercising and eating, there is the chance to dream. Turn off the TV, put away your phone and emails, look out of the window and dream.

In the privacy of your own mind you can dare to dream bigger. Inside your head, you are in the safest and most private place possible. No one can see in, no one can judge you and you can't fail. Use this freedom to connect with ideas and think big.

Let your thoughts wander - they don't have to be relevant to what you are doing work-wise. When you get stuck, stop. This is meant to be relaxing and fun, not a struggle.

Take a break, have a cup of tea or a walk, relax and come back to it. Chances are your mind will drift off while doing this. And this is when you start to come up with the best ideas.

"If you want creative workers, give them enough time to play"

John Cleese

www.BritishBusiness.School/BK0114

WEEK
15

BIG PLANET,
BIG IDEAS

When the early discoverers came back from the new world, they brought fantastical tales of mermaids, unicorns and leviathans that can eat a ship in one. Was it coincidence that these people were great storytellers?

They had seen all sorts of exciting and different things that gave them the basis of these tales. The unicorn has its basis in the narwhale (or possibly rhino), whose skull looks like a horse's with a massive spiral spike on top of it. Mermaids were manatees, or sea-cows and massive giant squid have been found, so why not even bigger and more formidable ones?

They told stories and came up with big ideas because they had seen more than others had. So you should too. This is not about being a great storyteller, it is about taking ideas and inspiration from other places and using them to help you come up with new ideas. You need to look at what is new and how to use it and not just in your own sphere. Take new technology and ideas and juxtapose them into a different markets or industries. Knowledge is power and the bigger your store of things that you can bring to bear, the better.

Travel and expose yourself to the world. The more adventurous can go to the ends of the earth, find out what others do and learn from them first-hand. This is much easier than before and the world is a smaller place than it used to be. But even if you can't travel, you have no excuse. With the internet, you can learn and observe other cultures and a myriad of global happenings from the comfort of your computer.

"Traveling- it leaves you speechless, then turns you into a storyteller"

Ibn Battuta

www.BritishBusiness.School/BK0115

WEEK
16

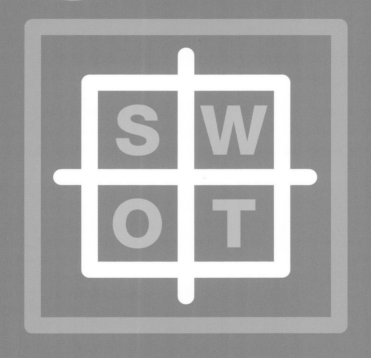

GOING OLD SCHOOL

A SWOT analysis is a key piece of marketing and management theory. It has been in use for a long time and with good reason. It can be a great starting point, especially if you are stuck or looking for a new edge.

Draw up a two-by-two grid and use a square each to list out your Strengths, Weaknesses, Opportunities and Threats. You instantly get a picture of where your brand or product is. It can be used in conjunction with all sorts of other grids and matrixes. You can map the competition, how adventurous your brand is, whether it offers quality/value for money and so on.

When you have this information, you can look at the gaps and work on big ideas to fill these. You can decide how to move it forward depending on what you want to achieve.

But stare hard at the gaps, these are the opportunities. What weaknesses can you build up and turn into strengths and what treats can you capitalise on and turn into opportunities?

"Build up your weaknesses until they become your strengths"

Knute Rockne

WEEK
17

PIG

ANGEL

CHICKEN

A BIT OF THIS, A BIT OF THAT

When I was a child, one of my favourite toys was a book full of different characters. There were a colourful selection of characters, male and female, human and animal. It was ring bound and cut laterally in three.

This allowed you to make up interesting new characters that might have a fireman's head, a doctor's body and the crocodile's legs. The Scotsman's kilt was always popular, but it let my young mind experiment with bringing together different elements to create something new.

The number of choices were restricted to a small mathematical possibility, but in real life there are endless possibilities.

There are so many different elements that can be combined together to create new and exciting ideas. Not all of them obviously live together and some of the most exciting new ideas come when people take things from very different fields and bring them together to make something really special.

"Normally, we do not so much look at things as overlook them"

Alan Watts

www.BritishBusiness.School/BK0117

THE HIGHER
GROUND

There are all sorts of areas that you can win at, even if you are not the biggest and the best. After all, there can only be one best.

As I am writing this section, **I am on a train going through a flooded landscape.** There is water all around, but we glide on through as we are on the higher ground.

What is your higher ground? What space do you or could you occupy to make you stand out?

Look at what can be conquered, but most of all, look for what has not yet been claimed.

Not everyone can be the biggest and best, but you can be the cleverest. Even if you are not the market leader, you can be the thought leader. Challenger brands are great at finding a niche they can own. Often the competition may be bigger or better in this area, but they have not claimed it. Are you faster, greener, more ethical or more subversive than your competition? Carve out a piece of mindspace and own it. When the flood of others comes, you will be the one standing out.

"If you would lift me up you must be on higher ground"

Ralph Waldo Emerson

WEEK
19

THE
MEDIUM
IS THE
MESSAGE

Sometimes, you just need to live the brand. The message that you are giving out is 'this is what we do and we love it'.

It's as true for a surf brand sitting on the beach with a driftwood fire as it is for a law firm in their wood-panelled office.

Use what you do and how you behave, to show that you are best of breed. Don't be ashamed of who you are; revel in it. It is the same with ideas. Sometimes a big idea can be about doing something in a way that lives your vaules so strongly, that the message is obvious. For example we delivered some phones for Kazam, a challenger brand with an underdog positioning.

The phones are for stores to trial and they are inside piñata dogs, wrapped in brown paper and string so you can see they are dogs, with Kazam the underdog stamped on them. Before you open up the package, you understand the product positioning. The medium is totally key to the message.

"The medium is the message"

Marshall McLuhan

www.BritishBusiness.School/BK0119

WEEK
20

i

i

i

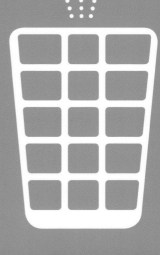

FILE 13

Sometimes an idea won't work, is not good enough for the situation, or will just be plain wrong for the audience.

The bin is an inviting place for a crumpled piece of paper. However, just because it did not work this time, does not mean it won't another time.

File 13 (the bin) should be kept at the back of your mind, or preferably written down. Many a time, I have used an element of an earlier idea that might have been turned down. It might be identical, it might be slightly changed or it might be just the essence, but a good idea is a good idea.

There are many reasons for a no and you might not always get the truth. People often want to protect your ego or let you down easily. Not enough budget, wrong for us, off brand and too risky, might be code for we plain don't like it.

But don't be disheartened, look at why you came up with the idea in the first place, the audience and outcomes. The chances are, it might be right for someone else down the line. Think of an idea as a patchwork quilt, it can have lots of different elements that make it up, some might be new, some might be reused, but the overall effect works.

"We all agree that your theory is crazy, but is it crazy enough?"

Niels Bohr

WEEK
21

The next three sections can be done together or taken one week at a time. They cover the planning, preparation and facilitation of brainstorming.

DOING STUFF WITH GROUPS

Big ideas and groups... it is going to happen. People love to get a group together for a brainstorm and to help thrash out some new ideas.

There are a few key things to do with a group to stop it descending into anarchy:

Take command

 Set the boundaries

 Have rules

Be a catalyst

 Get the group excited and the ideas flowing

 Record the output and set next steps

Without a leader, group sessions tend to become a confused and noisy mess, so it is important to take control and set the boundaries. This can be as simple as saying how long you are spending on various sections and what you will be doing.

It is a good idea to warm up the group, but this needs to be relevant to the audience. Not everyone wants an American style big-up with whooping and high fiving, but some will insist on it. One of my favourite ways to get a group, who have not met me, going is to talk about being opportunistic and I ask: Who here is opportunistic?

Most say they are, so I offer a £20 note to the first person to come and get it. It tends to take a while before someone takes it, then I ask the others how they feel about missing out. It tends to wake them up a bit.

With large groups, you need a bit of an iron fist in a cashmere glove, I personally feel 8 to 10 is the maximum number for a creative ideas session. You want to acknowledge everyone's thoughts and let people bounce ideas off each other, but someone needs to drive the direction and keep it moving. If your idea is dropped, let it go and come up with another one. If it is so good you can't let it go, wait till the end and talk to the decision maker. There may be something you could do slightly differently to make it work. The leader needs to be a catalyst who puts ideas together, encourages everyone and makes the whole greater than the sum of its parts.

"Think left and think right and think low and think high. Oh, the thinks you can think up if only you try!"

Dr. Seuss

www.BritishBusiness.School/BK0121

WEEK
22

A STORM IN
A TEACUP

Brainstorms should not be too stormy. They are meant to be fun and a great way to get the ideas flowing. Key to this is respect and I find the best thing is to have some rules and to get everyone to agree to stick to them. Put them up on the wall so they are visible.

Hold back negative judgment of ideas
Encourage wild and exaggerated ideas
Quantity counts at this stage, not quality
Build on the ideas put forward by others
Every person and every idea has equal worth

It is also very important to have a leader who can probe people, tease the ideas out and often more importantly park discussions if certain topics go on for too long. Especially if you are in a formal situation, it needs to be a bit different: jackets and ties off, sleeves rolled up. Have a scribe to write things up, capture your content and draw pictures where possible.

Introduce the topic and let people know what outputs you are hoping to have e.g. ideas for a film, or a new campaign. Talk through any key points, brand truths or core values. Get people to come up with ideas and call them out, then put them up on the board. Then look at the ones people like and start working deeper into them. Move ideas around on a wall to group and cluster them into natural groups to create campaigns. When you get quiet periods, get people to swap ideas and build on other people. When you wrap up, divide stuff into the really good stuff, the interesting and the not so good. Photograph it, collect everything and write up the notes. Circulate this with your next steps and don't forget to thank everyone for their input.

"There are some things you can only learn in a storm"
Joel Olsteen

www.BritishBusiness.School/BK0122

WEEK
23

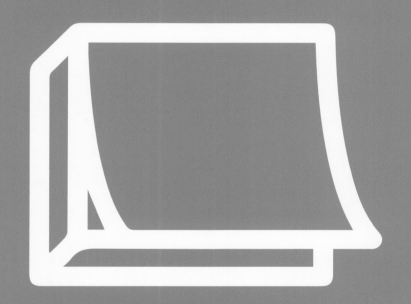

PRESSURE
TECHNIQUE

The first stage of a brainstorm is to get lots of ideas down. Good or bad, it is all about volume and you should not judge the ideas, the more the merrier. But sometimes, people are a bit reticent and don't want to join in. The session looks like it will never start and no one is stepping forward to get the ball rolling. You need some action and you need the ideas to start flowing.

Give the team a pack of PostIt™ notes and tell them they each need to come up with five themes for the idea in five minutes. They can be anything and nothing will be laughed at. But they must have at least five and if they can do more, that is brilliant.

The first few ideas will be the obvious ones, but once people are put under a little pressure and stretched to go beyond that, they will start thinking of other things. Get them up on a wall and start to group them. You then go through these ideas and sort them in to great ideas, ones that need more work and ones to park for now.

Then look at how the ideas can work together, one thing might be weak, but combine it with another, and it might really work well. The session is under way.

Pressure makes people join in and even if their ideas are not great, it gets them thinking. The other benefit of getting people to write things down, is that everyone joins in and everyone's ideas are heard, even if they are shy and retiring. If you just get people to shout things out, you will find a few people will dominate the conversation and you can miss some great ideas.

"A diamond is a chunk of coal that did well under pressure"
Henry Kissinger

C.
DEVELOPING
THE IDEA

"I never made one of my discoveries through the process of rational thinking"

Albert Einstein

WEEK
24

PUSHING
THE DIP

Have you ever wondered what makes the difference between good and great?

It's often not very much, but the people who create great tend to keep pushing that little bit more. That last 5% or 10% that makes all the difference. For some it is about creating an utterly perfect product that people love. For others it is about not giving up when the going gets tough. You will never know how many steps away you are from the top of the mountain, the great people always give it one more push. It applies across the board from how you implement, who you offer your product to, how you sell and market it. Is there an area that you know needs a bit more of a push?

Seth Godin has written many excellent books and one of my favourites, 'The Dip' is about when to quit. The core message is that many people fail without knowing how close they were to success, while others slog away when they should have given up a long time ago.

Often, when times are really hard, you might just be one big push away from success. So lift up your head, keep on pushing, revel in the challenge and believe that you can make it with one more big push, it will often make a huge difference.

"Never quit something with great long-term potential just because you can't deal with the stress of the moment"

Seth Godin

www.BritishBusiness.School/BK0124

WEEK
25

POSITIVITY IS EVERYTHING

One of the key things when coming up with big ideas is positivity. You need to keep going and keep pushing; if you do this day in, day out, it can wear you down. There will be blocks and times when your mind is empty. When this happens, change track, change location and get others to chip in. Distract and disturb. It helps if you have someone to bounce ideas off. But you need positivity to keep going.

I really do believe that:
'It's going to be great' and, funnily enough, it generally is.

Pessimism is infectious – much more so than positivity or good leadership. Cut out the bad stories and the emotional drains, revel in the positive and know that your ideas are going to be amazing.

Things will always go wrong along the way; it is how you react to and solve these problems that make you who you are. There will be good times and there will be bad times. Positivity will get you out of the holes and allow you to get back on track. People can smell defeat and pessimism. The business pitch where you are so desperate that you are willing to beg is one you will probably lose. Despair is unattractive to clients and staff alike, and is contagious.

Believe in your ideas, but don't fool yourself. Some will need to be parked and put in file 13, but when you believe in an idea, give it your all and spread the positivity.

"Once you replace negative thoughts with positive ones, you'll start having positive results"

Willie Nelson

WEEK
26

HORSES
FOR
COURSES

All sorts of people want big ideas and want to benefit from the energy they bring. But what works for an aggressive consumer start-up will not be appropriate for a big corporate. They won't buy it and if they do, chances are, it won't work.

So ideas need to fit the client and be relevant to their market.

I love working for start-ups and challenger brands that take risks and are up for fun stuff. But they are not the only people out there. More conservative companies and industries have their benefits too. For one, it is easier to make them look good and bring about a significant uplift in creativity. But you need to be careful as change in some cases needs to be incremental. A small change might seem massive for a conservative company.

On the flip side, your idea might be a world-beater and create a monumental shift, pushing the client or product way beyond the competition. But if you are working with someone who is already a world-beater, like Apple, you are going to have to work very hard to make a difference. Which isn't to say I wouldn't like to give it a go...

So work out what you need and balance the level of creativity and out-thereness to your industry, its norms and levels. Don't feel you have to be more conservative than the competition, but do bear in mind that you need to be in the right ball park.

"Not all who wander are lost"

J.R.R.Tolkien

www.BritishBusiness.School/BK0126

WEEK
27

MESSAGE IN
A BOTTLE

Congratulations, you are half way through. This week is a chance to stop and reflect on what is working and what is not. Look at what you want to keep doing and how you are going to keep doing it, to change the way you work for the better.

Look back over your worksheets and see what worked for you and how it is going to work going forward.

Write yourself three letters, one to be read in a month, one to be read in six months and one to be read in a year.

Put down how you are going to work differently and the steps you have learned that you are going to continue to implement. Also write down your commitments to yourself of what you are going to do differently, milestones you want to achieve and when you are going to complete them by. Don't forget the carrot, so look at the reward you would like to give yourself when you hit these objectives.

Seal them up and put them away. You can give them to a friend to post to you, or lock them away, but no peaking, they need to remain un-opened until their time arrives.

"Believe you can and you're halfway there"
Theodore Roosevelt

www.BritishBusiness.School/BK0127

WEEK
28

WE DON'T KNOW WHAT WE ARE DOING

A lot of people live in their comfort zone. If you want to create a big idea that makes a difference, you can't do that. You need to step outside.

A lot of the things we propose have not been done before or not in this way. Sometimes, we can honestly say that we don't know what we are doing.

But (and it is a big but) someone will. We live in a very connected, globalised world and there is unprecedented access to global talent. This means you can reach out to your existing network or find new people to do almost anything.

Don't be afraid of the implementation: someone will be able to do it. And the harder it looks to implement, the chances are that it might just be something really spectacular. When you think of Felix Baumgartnew parked on the edge of space about to parachute down, you can see the amazing things that can be done, surely your project is not that hard. Think big and worry about how to implement the idea later.

"The only thing standing between you and your goal is the bullshit story you keep telling yourself as to why you can't achieve it"

Jordan Belfort

WEEK
29

AMPLIFYING YOUR MESSAGES

Big ideas are a loud hailer. Your core message might be a small and delicate thing, but the big idea can help you amplify this message and get it out there.

You need to look at the best ways to amplify this and who you want to amplify it to. There is no point shouting at an empty room, or talking at length to the wrong people. Use the communication streams used by the people you want to influence.

This makes it much easier to make some noise and to get yourself heard. Look at who influences your target market and get them to push it for you. Each generation and group has their heroes, the people they go to for knowledge and who they trust. These people can have a huge reach and enormous power. Get them on your side and get them to make a big difference.

Once you have chosen your medium and with the help of the right influencers, you will start to gather some momentum. Soon you will reach a critical moment when your message takes on a life of its own.

"The humblest individual experts some influence, either for good or evil, upon others"

Henry Ward Beecher

www.BritishBusiness.School/BK0129

WEEK
30

FIVE STAR QUALITY, CHEAP AS CHIPS

At the end of the day, we need to sell our ideas, but can people afford them? **Value is not about price. It's about how something changes your life.** A rush to the bottom to make everything as cheap as possible is not good for your business and not good for the client.

Commoditisation goes to the lowest common denominator and reduces value. Something that costs a million pounds but makes ten million is great value. But a ten thousand pound project that has no impact is a waste of money.

In the airline industry, business class survived the recession by offering the value of getting you to your meeting fresh after a proper sleep. So it's not always about the bottom line. Some people believe that 'from the moment an idea is worth having, no one cares about the cost', but at the end of the day, you have to persuade someone to pay for it. And that is all about the value created.

You will be challenged on cost for ideas, but remember what value is: the output, not the amount of money it costs. Creativity is the best way to maximise budgets and when people are pushed to the edge, the most creative examples arise.

So avoid a rush to the bottom and commoditisation, use creativity to give yourself the edge, one which people will be willing to pay for.

"Price is what you pay, value is what you get"

Warren Buffet

WEEK
31

WHAT DO YOU WANT OUT OF AN IDEA?

For me, there are three key things that will help make an idea successful.
It needs to either:
Attract, involve or reward.
Preferably all three.

Attracting is all about getting people's attention. If they don't know about the idea, it will fail.

Involving is about getting them to interact with the idea and this is where we communicate the key messages and create a lasting memory.

Rewarding is to make it worth their while. This is not a bribe and I have purposely not put this in as an attractor. This is about giving people information that makes things better or allows them to leave having had a worthwhile interaction. If they are not happy to have interacted, all else is in vain.

If you shout in a crowded place, people will look at you, but they will soon turn away and forget you. Shout again and they will ignore you. You need to make sure your target market voluntarily give you their attention and remember you for the right reasons. If you have at least one of these three, people will pay attention.

"Where there is shouting, there is no true knowledge"
Leonardo de Vinci

www.BritishBusiness.School/BK0131

WEEK
32

SHOW ME
YOURS

Ideas abhor a vacuum, you need to share and bounce ideas around. You need to compare and contrast. **Look at what is out there for what you are trying to do. Who is doing it best and how are they different?** Also look in different markets and areas.

If you are interested in being the best at service, look at who are the leaders in other categories, not just your own.

It's not just ideas that like company, you do as well. Find someone who you can bounce your ideas off, important tip; they need to be honest.

There will be times when your ideas are not right and you get over excited and too attached to them, only an honest sounding board who you can trust, will be able to persuade you to drop it when you really love it.

It is not just about keeping you honest, when you share ideas and kick them around a bit, they tend to get better, people add better bits and you get rid of the rough edges and things that you should probably have changed yourself.

"The good ideas will survive"

Quentin Tarantino

WEEK
33

FIRST MOVER
DISADVANTAGE

When you are working on a big idea, there comes a time when you have to bring it to life and make it happen. This might be something totally new, or something similar may have already been done. Both have their positives and negatives.

If it has been done before, this is not the end of the world. There is no such thing as an original idea; most are developments of other ideas and a new way of putting things together. Luxury watch brands frequently use big glossy adverts in lifestyle magazines. It is not a big idea, but it must work for them as they are there month after month (although I am dying for them to do something more creative). But if you were launching a new watch, it might be that this is an essential part of your strategy.

So what if it has not been done before? There might be a very good reason. It could be that it is impossible and doomed to fail. But don't let that get you down, it might not have worked previously, but with advances in technology etc, you might be able to do new things that will make it work.

First mover advantage is great, but sometimes you have to educate the whole market about something new and take all the development work on your shoulders.

Often it is better to be just behind the cutting edge and make use of other people's efforts. But most of all, the biggest challenge is to make it happen. Too often people see a successful idea and say they thought of that, but didn't do anything about it.

It is up to the entrepreneurs to make these things happen and bring them to life. People often worry about not being able to protect their ideas. The way to win here is be first and be best. If you are any good, people will copy and come after you, but this is just a compliment. Don't go chasing around trying to beat the competition, make them come after you, especially if they are bigger.

"When people say, "I could have done that", I say, "Yes, you could. But you didn't. And I did"

Tom Stoppard

D.
SELLING THE IDEA

" *Sell a man a fish, he eats for a day, teach a man how to fish, you ruin a wonderful business opportunity* "

Karl Marx

WEEK
34

LET ME
TAKE YOU
ON A
JOURNEY

Selling-in a big idea is an involved process. I like to do it face to face and talk it through. Just emailing over our ideas, is to me, throwing them away.

Unless there is a specific reason, if someone cannot make time to meet you and listen to your ideas, they do not value them or you anyway. The flip side of this is that when we do present, it needs to be compelling and you need to get complete buy in.

I like to take people on a journey. A journey of discovery, where the idea is introduced, built up and talked through. A journey with a beginning, a middle and an end. I take my time and build up to the idea. Don't give it as a throwaway line, you need to introduce it so it is an exciting and interesting thing that people are fascinated by.

The journey gives you time to show your belief and enthusiasm in the idea. If you don't love it, then there is very little chance that others will either.

By the end of the journey, it becomes their idea and it feels like they have discovered it for themselves, which is always a great step to acceptance and commitment to the idea.

" Find Joy in the Journey"

Thomas S. Monson

www.BritishBusiness.School/BK0134

WEEK
35

SEVEN
STORIES

If you talk to actors and especially writers, they will tell you that there are only seven stories and all tales, from all of time come from these.

TRAGEDY	COMEDY	OVERCOMING THE MONSTER	VOYAGE AND RETURN

QUEST (OR JOURNEY)	RAGS TO RICHES	REBIRTH

Once you know these building blocks, you can tell any story. But hopefully your business is neither a comedy nor a tragedy. You need to look at your building blocks. What are your stories? They can be pretty simple. E.G. if you sell breakfast cereal, they could be:

Overcoming the monster becomes the fight against the competition, overcoming them through messages about healthier ingredients and a tastier product. Rebirth could be a new use of the product, e.g. using it for snacking or dieting. And Voyage and return could be an improved product or new formula. Something trusted that is now a bit better and worth trying.

This covers most of the possible stories that can be told about the product. It might be that you are talking about added iron, a better flavour or collecting tokens, but the main activity will always feed into one of these stories.

Advertisers talk a lot about product truths, things that they want people to know about products as fact. The consumer may not always agree with these and it is the advert's job to persuade them, but whatever the truth, it will need to be rooted in one of the key stories.

All marketers are storytellers, and the more you know about stories and how to tell them, the better you will be.

www.BritishBusiness.School/BK0135

"Great stories happen to those who can tell them"

Ira Glass

WEEK
36

A PICTURE IS WORTH A THOUSAND WORDS

Pictures are very valuable for big ideas. Many a big idea has been ignored or turned down because people didn't get it. **Where possible we use visualisers to bring ideas to life. There is a huge sense of pride when we see what started off as a picture come to life.** If it looks like the initial sketch, we know we have protected our big idea and driven something through.

Pictures don't need to be amazing - they can be very basic. In these days of digital media, it is great to see people still sketching on the backs of napkins and menus. Whether pen on paper or stylus on glass, sketching something always brings it to life.

A lot of people are scared of sketching, but you should not be. The key is to break it down into simple building blocks. If you can draw a square, a circle and a triangle, you can add these together to do a lot of different things.

Use these simple beginnings to form your picture. Don't worry about the detail, give the outline and go from there. A bit of shading helps a lot. Think what direction the light is coming from and colour in a bit of shading on the opposite side. Perspective is easier than it looks and works by fixing a couple of lines on the horizon and linking every line to there. Have a stylised person who you always draw - I use a circle with a triangle squiggle below, not much like a person, but it works.

Before you know it, you have a picture coming together. A small amount of skill goes a long way and while I am no Leonardo, I can get my ideas across. If you are not a sketcher, there are hundreds of free online tutorials that will give you the basics in a few hours and I highly recommend giving them a go. For those who really don't want to draw pictures, try making your words more visual. By writing key words down and showing how they link together, you can describe the available options and what you want to do. Use boxes, circles and arrows to bring it all together.

"I prefer drawing to talking. Drawing is faster and leaves less room for lies"
Le Corbusier

WEEK
37

A PROP IS
WORTH
10,000
WORDS

If a picture is worth 1,000 words, then surely a prop is worth 10,000. A lot of people are not able to visualise ideas and solutions. A drawing can be a big help here, but a prop can be even more useful. Having something that you can get your hands on sets you apart from the competition.

They are not just for explaining - they can be used to introduce. As an ice-breaker for a big pitch, I got everyone to bring an item that represented their passions outside the office. When we introduced ourselves and talked through why we had brought a certain object with us, we showed our whole personalities.

We use it as a proof point for big ideas and to show that we get a key idea or how a company thinks. With Lidl we gave them a delicious fudge I had made from ingredients purchased in their store. This showed not only how their high quality ingredients can make delicious food, but how massively cheaper they are than buying the ingredients from other supermarkets.

So make sure that your props are there for a purpose and that they bring your ideas to life, or show how you understand what you are talking about.

"Show the readers everything, tell them nothing"

Ernest Hemingway

www.BritishBusiness.School/BK0137

WEEK
38

KEEP IT
SIMPLE
STUPID

KISS is an old adage, it has its detractors, but there is a certain truth in it. A really big idea, a true eureka moment, should be simple in its explanation, if not its implementation.

You should get it straight away and without long explanation. If you have to explain it and get repeated questions because people don't get it, the chances are it is not a big idea, or you are not communicating it well. **It is like a joke: if you have to explain it, it is simply not funny.**

A big idea can be hard to sell, especially if it is entirely new. Henry Ford pioneered the affordable car. He had to sell a totally new product to a new audience who did not know they wanted it yet. His really big idea was the manufacturing process that made it all possible, but to the public, he was selling the automotive dream at an affordable price.

So you might understand what you are talking about, but do others? Test your pitch with your market, get feedback and make it better. Test and adjust, test and adjust until you have something that people can understand straight away.

"Simplicity is the ultimate sophistication"
Leonardo de Vinci

WEEK

39.

HANGING
ON

Coming up with and implementing ideas is hard work.

'Computer says no,' is far too common and people will push back and stop you doing things, especially if it is new or untried. People will always fight against the different and strange, not to mention the problems of not-invented-here syndrome. It is hard, but you need to hang on in there and keep pushing. There is always a point where you need to let go, but it needs to be judged finely. You need to have the right degree of tenacity for the right situation.

With sales, I tend to go for more of a: 'It's not no until they call security' approach. When sourcing new ways of doing things and implementing ideas, you need the same drive to get people onside and understand that there is another way of doing things.

But when presenting ideas to clients, you need a much more flexible approach. After all, they are the experts in their field and with their audience.

You also need to be realistic. Is the idea worth holding out for? Was it the best solution you could put forward? You can't be at your best all the time, if you are, you are mediocre by definition.

Even the best have off days, but they balance this with days of genius. Accept that you won't always be at your best - but when you are, that is when you can make a big difference. So fight for the great ideas and people will come round eventually.

"If at first you don't succeed, try, try again. Then quit. No use being a damn fool about it"

W.C. Fields

www.BritishBusiness.School/BK0139

WEEK
40

IS
SOMETIMES
THE
KINDEST
WORD

Occasionally, we can go a bit too far and what we propose seems much more extreme than what clients were expecting.

Often, a mix up in the briefing can be the problem. For example, if they ask for something to be a bit more "out-there", they might be thinking of bright coloured table cloths, while we are starting to build remote control seagulls and to launch their competition with rockets (literally).

Over time with clients you get to work out the right level, but especially in an early stage of relationships, no's can be very helpful.

A 'no' can be the start of some more detailed communication, so it's often a good thing. By finding out what does not work, you can go in a new direction that might and you may end up with something even better. Embrace the no: it takes you one step closer to the yes.

The second part of embracing the no is that ideas are often hybrids. They are a bit of this, a bit of that and a twist of the other. A no idea on its own might be too much (or not enough), but it might work along with another idea.

"The art of leadership is saying no, not saying yes. It is very easy to say yes"

Tony Blair

www.BritishBusiness.School/BK0140

WEEK
41

COMPLACENCY
KILLS

Familiarity can breed contempt and nothing becomes more familiar than the relationship between a client and an agency on a retainer. **Some agencies are lucky enough to have very long-term relationships with clients.** They know the brand guidelines inside out and they know what ideas are likely to be chosen. When it goes too far, complacency can slip in. The creativity has gone and the ideas become mundane. They think they are doing them a favour, but in reality they are not.

It is important to break out of this. Sure, the brand restrictions are important, but if you are playing too safe, you will never innovate. **Brands will always flex for brilliant ideas and you won't find these if you never go looking.** *You also put yourself at risk from those who are still free to think big ideas.*

Think how this applies to you when you are thinking about big ideas. Do you automatically say no to things because you know they won't work or you feel a key stakeholder won't like them? Go to a different location, take away the rules and the barriers, forget your pre-conceptions and get back to basics.

This might generate some wild ideas, but they can be refined to be made relevant. At the very least you will have refreshed your approach and improved your relationships.

"Complacency is a state of mind that exists only in retrospective: it has to be shattered before being ascertained"

Vladimir Nabokov

www.BritishBusiness.School/BK0141

WEEK 42

1

2

3

THREE IDEAS

One of my pet hates is when people ask for three ideas, so they can choose. Why three ideas? De la Soul might consider it the magic number, but why should we? Often people come up with two and then scrape together a bad third to make up the numbers.

More often than not, this idea gets chosen and the process starts from the weakest point. Never put in a space filler, a weaker idea is often chosen by committee when people end up going for the safest most boring idea.

Believe in your ideas. We never come back with three ideas unless we have three we believe in. Sometimes we do two, four, or even just one if we are that passionate about it. Go for quality every time. If you live by your convictions and are confident about them, others will be as well and they will follow.

"3…That's the magic number"
De la Soul

www.BritishBusiness.School/BK0142

WEEK 43

WHAT ARE YOU GOING TO DO BY WHEN?

Getting started is often the hardest step: to commit to starting, to say you are going to do it, to put your head above the parapet. A timeline is often a good way to get started. **Working back from launch date will give you an idea of when you need to start,** and putting a line in the sand will let you know when you have started.

But if we only say this to ourselves, it is all too easy to let dates slide. Why not make it public? Why not shout it out to the world? I often motivate myself by telling others what I am going to do, so I then have to do it.

This can be as simple as committing a date to a client, your colleagues or letting friends know. Never underestimate the importance of timings when selling in an idea. Especially if it is creative or scary, a timeline will reassure people and help you to deliver on time.

Critical path analysis can be a bit technical, but the core elements of key activities and actions that need doing before others are all worth noting. Add key deadlines such as print and lead times to your timeline so everyone knows what needs doing when, to achieve the project. It is a great shame to see a big idea fall to pieces because it can't be delivered on time, breaking it down into manageable chunks makes it much more achievable.

"If you do what you've always done, you'll get what you've always gotten"

Tony Robbins

E.
GETTING EVERYONE ELSE ON BOARD

"It is amazing what you can accomplish if you do not care who gets the credit"

Harry S Truman

THANK YOU ISN'T THE HARDEST WORD

When you have a group of people bringing a big idea to life, it is hard work and can be very time consuming. **So make sure people know that you value their input.**

Thank you: *such a simple phrase, but a largely underused one. For me, it is the most basic of management tools. It takes seconds to say and if from the heart can make a big difference. Punctuality may be the manners of princes, but thank you is the manners of men. Apart from being common courtesy, it shows you value others as themselves and for their work. Say it regularly and mean it when you say it.*

"I can no other answer make but thanks and thanks, and ever thanks..."
William Shakespeare

WEEK
45

THREE STEPS TO CHANGE THE WORLD

Big ideas need people who are going to make them happen. Big ideas often involve change and take people into areas they have not been before. The people who implement them are key - if they fail, you fail, and the idea might flounder and die.

There are three things that people need to make it happen:

Pride in what
they are doing

Confidence
to do it

Desire to make
change happen

They need management to back them up and support so they are not on their own, but change can and will happen. The world can be changed.

Think big, see what you can do to change the world. Where possible, for internal projects, we use a company's own people to help bring things to life. By involving colleagues of the people you are trying to influence, you will find it easier to spread the pride, confidence and desire.

"Do, or do not. There is no 'try"

Yoda

F.
THE BIGGER PICTURE, ALL ABOUT YOU

*"Attitude is a little
thing that makes
a big difference"*
Winston Churchill

WEEK
46

WHAT MOVES YOU?

Morning comes, the alarm screams at you and you have to move from the warm welcoming embrace of bed. When it is cold and dark outside, what makes you throw the duvet to one side and jump out of bed?

We all need motivation to get moving and make stuff happen, but it is not the same for everyone.

Some do it to make a point: Lamborghini 'only' made tractors until the founder was insulted by Enzo Ferrari, so he started making luxury cars to show he could. Some lust for money, some for power and others just want recognition. Work out what motivates you and this will enable you to focus on achieving it.

Some people are goal orientated and have a book of rewards they will give themselves when they achieve things and some are more altruistic. The key thing is being true to yourself, there is no point in lying and no one else needs to know.

"If you want something you've never had, you must be willing to do something you've never done"

Thomas Jefferson

www.BritishBusiness.School/BK0146

WEEK
47

A BIG IDEA HELPS YOU WORK, REST AND PLAY

I feel that creativity can be brought to bear on all aspects of your life. **You can come up with big ideas that transform your home life as well as your business life** and what could be more important?

A new way of working might give you more time with your loved ones and make you more productive, a win-win.

The hardest step is often working out what it is you want to achieve. What are your goals? Are you motivated by money or lifestyle? Like most people it might be somewhere in-between.You would love to be paid buckets of cash, but would rather be chilling out on a beach where you would be lucky to get buckets of crabs. Setting realistic goals will make you more likely to achieve them, but remember that realistic does not have to mean low or boring goals. What does success look like to you?

"Success is getting what you want; happiness is wanting what you get"
Dale Carnegie

www.BritishBusiness.School/BK0147

WEEK
48

DON'T BE
A CHEESE
MONGER

There is an old business fable about a cheesemonger. **He spends so long getting all of the details of his business set up** just how he wants them, that he forgets he has a cellar full of cheese. He does not get round to selling the cheese and it all goes off. The moral of the story is that sometimes, you just need to get on with it.

With big ideas, you need to get the ball rolling and try things out. This is very close to my heart and I believe very strongly in more testing and less debating. Even the best ideas need some adjustment and refinement, but they need to see the light of day. Get some real feedback, but more importantly, make something happen.

Having someone who takes responsibility is key to this. There might be failures along the way, but you need to fast forward to fail. If it is not going to work, be ready to ditch that and start a new one. Fear of failure will lead to inactivity and often, ironically, failure itself.

93% of businesses that succeed don't continue with their original business strategy. But if they never started, then they would never succeed. You need to stay nimble, but you do need to ship. Seth Godin says this best: "Don't worry if you don't think what you ship is good enough. It is. The scarce part is the shipping."

"Whatever you can do, or dream you can do, begin it. Boldness has genius, power and magic in it"
Johann Wolfgang von Goethe

WEEK
49

ONE LIFE, LIVE IT

The most successful people I have met are all passionate about what they do. It might be work, but they love it and it drives them forward. This passion shows. Clients and colleagues can see it; it inspires those they lead and it drives clients to buy.

I don't think you can fake this, nor should you, as you are only fooling yourself. You should be interested in what you do, or move to what interests you. Look for your angle or speciality. It might not be far from where you are and need not be a wholesale lifestyle change.

We spend so much of our lives at work. The majority of us look at a screen for longer than we sleep every day. Some passion in what you do is essential for being the best.

If you are passionate about your job, you will enjoy it more, perform better and rise to the top faster. Ideas can help with this. Creating big ideas is fun and if you fill your work with big ideas and innovation, you will be more passionate about it. What is your passion? What do you enjoy at work and what is the most profitable. If you can do more of what you enjoy and are best at, you will be better.

"You only live once, but if you do it right, once is enough"

Mae West

WEEK
50

ROLL
WITH THE
PUNCHES

Every dog has his day. Sometimes everything is going your way and you can't put a foot wrong.

Use that energy: call everyone, take the risks, do the things you were worried about and give it a go.

Amazingly, it often works. People can hear the positivity in your voice and sense the energy inside you. This has a snowball effect and can lead to great things.

The flipside is also true. If it is all falling to pieces, it is hard to make that important call and your negativity booms down the phone. You have to pick yourself up and push back hard on yourself so you can still perform. Take a break and try to re-energise yourself. If that does not work, do the admin jobs and other tasks that need doing.

At least make good use of the time when you are not at your best. Realise this is not the time and work on how you are going to pick yourself up and come back firing on all cylinders. It is up to you to make today a good day and if you can't do that, make sure tomorrow is.

"What day is it?" asked Pooh "It's today," squeaked Piglet. "My favourite day," said Pooh"

A.A.Milne

WEEK
51

BLAME SOMEONE ELSE AND GET ON WITH YOUR LIFE

Ok, I don't really mean blame someone else, but the message is important. Ideas don't always work or won't be picked up. Get over it.

This happens a lot and does not mean that your ideas are not intrinsically good ones.

It might be the wrong time, the wrong place or the wrong application. The key is to take on board that this time, that idea is not working or not going to happen. So focus your energies on making the next one better.

"Don't spend time beating on a wall, hoping to transform it into a door"

Coco Chanel

www.BritishBusiness.School/BK0151

WEEK
52

WRAPPING
IT UP

Well done, you have made it to the end.

Six months ago, you sent yourself a letter, it is time to open it and see how you are doing. Have you hit your objectives and are you on track?

Look through your worksheet notes and see what has been of the biggest impact to you from this course.

You have a letter waiting for you in six months time and now is the time to do another for six months and a year away. This means you will have two for six months time and you will be able to compare how you have grown and got better in the last six months as you compare one to the other.

Hopefully you have enjoyed this book and the difference it has made to you. Dip into it again from time to time to refresh your knowledge or consider passing it on to someone else.

"Now this is not the end. It is not even the beginning of the end. But it is, perhaps, the end of the beginning"

Winston Churchill

NOTES

"Tom is the ultimate 'ideas man', when he enters a room his infectious energy has the ability to spark ideas from the most unlikely places. This fantastic book guides you through his process and demonstrates how to implement it in a manageable way, it's as good as having him in the room...Well almost!"

James Atkins, CMO, Kazam

Fun, playful, insightful and full of charm - encouraging businesses to systematically re-visit often overlooked areas. I love the concept and found myself utterly immersed."

James Hughes, Head of Marketing and Communications, Edmiston

"A brilliantly creative insightful book with lots of practical ideas and wisdom for everyone involved in the business of marketing. It's a book I wish I'd written!"

Roger Draper, CEO, Warrington Wolves

"It's All About The Idea is an essential manual for guiding you through the delicate process of idea generation through to execution. Great ideas are fragile and sensitive, this book provides you with the practical steps to ensure you don't destroy them along the way. Common sense for creativity, a companion for life."

Phill Jones, MD, Motors.co.uk

"Tom Tuke-Hastings is the master of creativity, in this book he combines great situational and business awareness and shows that any challenge can be overcome, if we sit back and take some time to think outside the box."

Steve Fraser, Managing Director, United Utilities

"Simple, clear and inspiring: like having your creative fairy sitting on your shoulder reminding you what you need to do to keep the ideas coming"

Louise Fowler, Marketing Director, First Direct